I Can DRAW Animals

P9-DEX-066

Cover illustrated by Renée Daily

Interiors illustrated by Yuri Salzman

Here's what you need...

You're about to become an artist! Before you start, make sure you have a pencil, a pencil sharpener, an eraser, a felt-tip pen, and one or more of the different types of media pictured here. Then, look in the back of the book for your grid pages. They'll help you to follow the special drawing steps. If you need more paper, you can ask a grownup to help you to copy them.

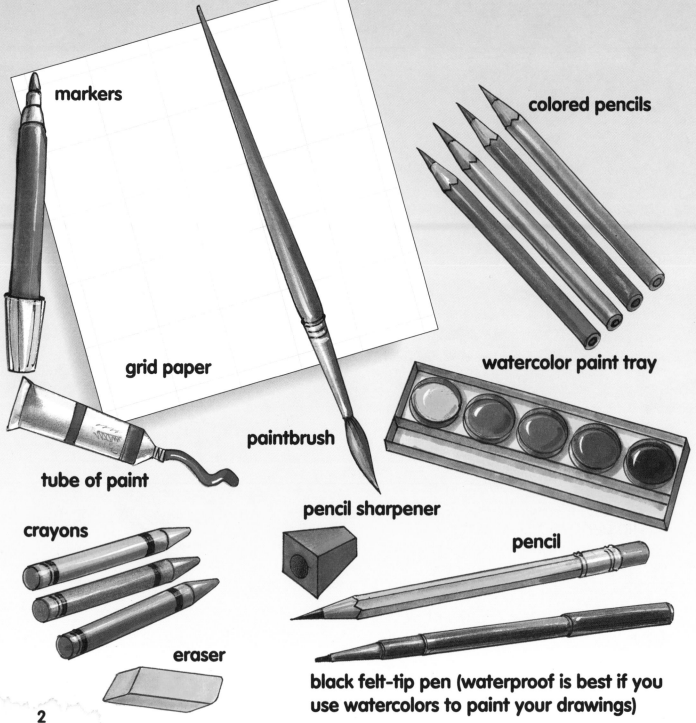

markers

colored pencils

grid paper

watercolor paint tray

paintbrush

tube of paint

pencil sharpener

crayons

pencil

eraser

black felt-tip pen (waterproof is best if you use watercolors to paint your drawings)

2

And here's what you do!

1 Copy each step-by-step drawing onto your grid paper, noticing where the drawing should touch the lines on your grid. Draw lightly in pencil. Since each new step is shown in blue, you'll always know exactly what to do next.

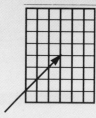

TIP: Be sure to start in the middle of the grid paper.

2 When you've drawn all the steps shown in blue, use your felt-tip pen to trace over the pencil lines you need to keep, then erase all the extra pencil lines.

Now you have a perfect drawing to color any way you'd like! Before you color, you may want to read pages 30 - 32 for some extra coloring tips.

Penguin

Follow the numbered drawing steps. The blue lines show each new step you will need to draw.

1 Draw a circle and an oval for the head and the body. Add wings and feet.

2 Add an eye, a beak, face detail, and lines for shoulders.

3 Use your felt-tip pen to trace over the lines you want to keep, and erase the extra pencil lines.

4 Color your penguin!

4

Bear

Draw the body and head. Add legs and an ear. Draw a snout and an eye.

1

Add the rest of the ear, another leg and paws.

2

Use your felt-tip pen to trace over the lines you want to keep, and erase the extra pencil lines.

3

If you leave your bear white, he can be a polar bear!

4 Color your bear!

5

Deer

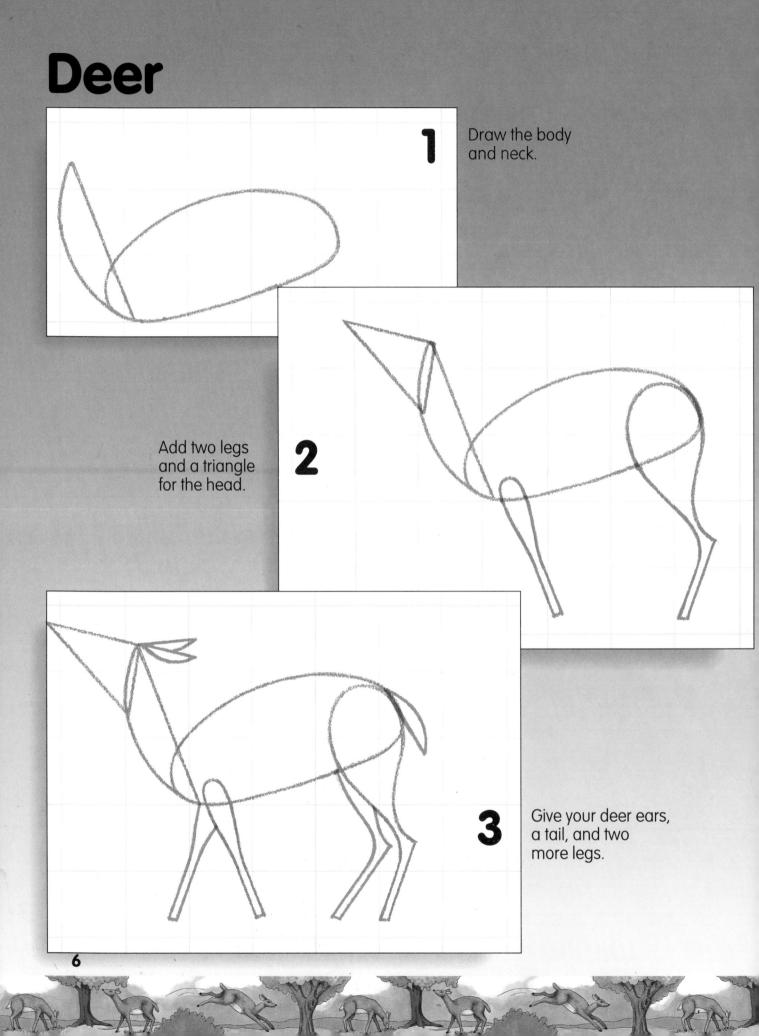

1 Draw the body and neck.

2 Add two legs and a triangle for the head.

3 Give your deer ears, a tail, and two more legs.

4 Add four hooves and an eye. Use curved lines to define the head and body.

Later, you'll find out how to make your deer run and jump!

Use your felt-tip pen to trace over the lines you want to keep, and erase the extra pencil lines.

5

6 Color your deer!

Frog

Draw an oval for the body. Add eyes, a mouth, and legs.

1

2 Add forelegs. Use circles to draw the eyelids and curved lines to draw the face.

3 Add lines for feet.

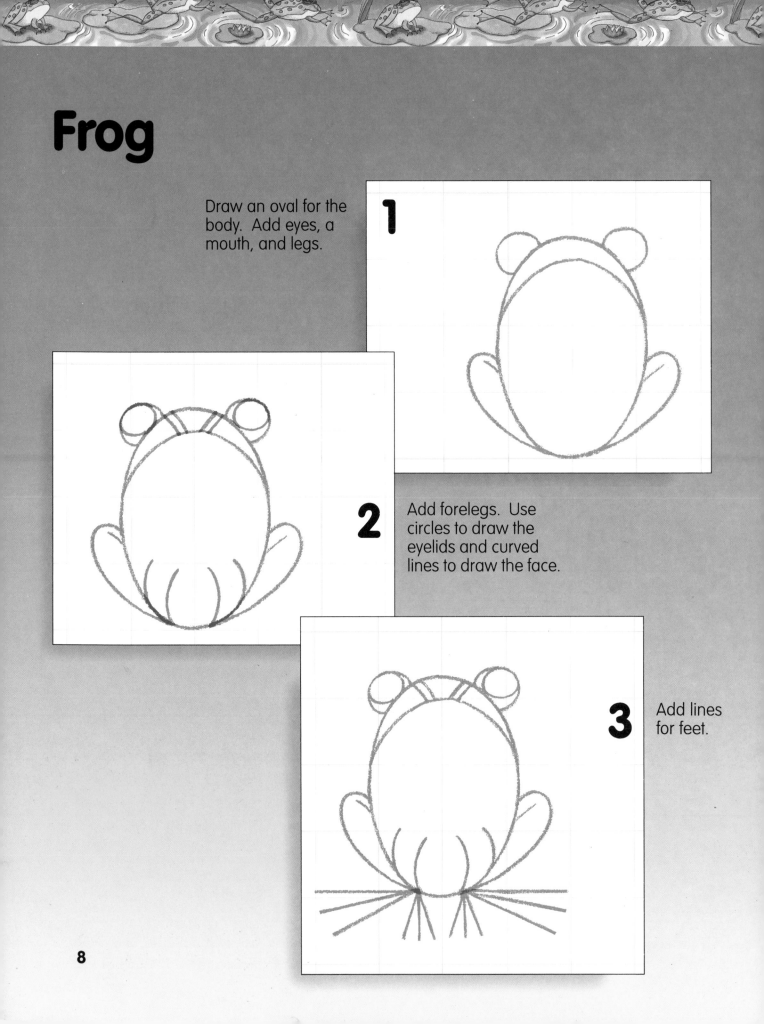

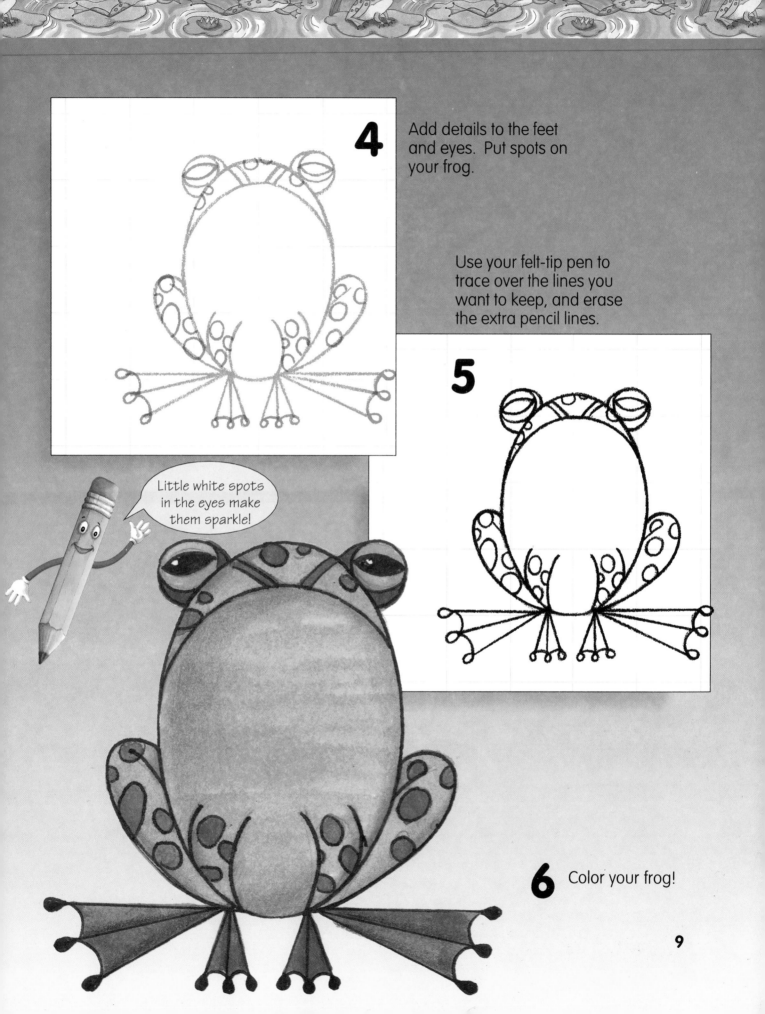

4 Add details to the feet and eyes. Put spots on your frog.

Use your felt-tip pen to trace over the lines you want to keep, and erase the extra pencil lines.

5

Little white spots in the eyes make them sparkle!

6 Color your frog!

Animals in Action

You can make your animals move by changing the positions of their legs.

You can use the same shapes you used to draw the front of your frog to draw the back of him as he jumps.

When the frog is leaping, his hind legs are stretched out behind him. (Learn how to draw a frog on page 8.)

To make the deer run, draw two legs stretched out, and two legs bent up close to the deer's body. (Learn how to draw a deer on page 6.)

Monkey

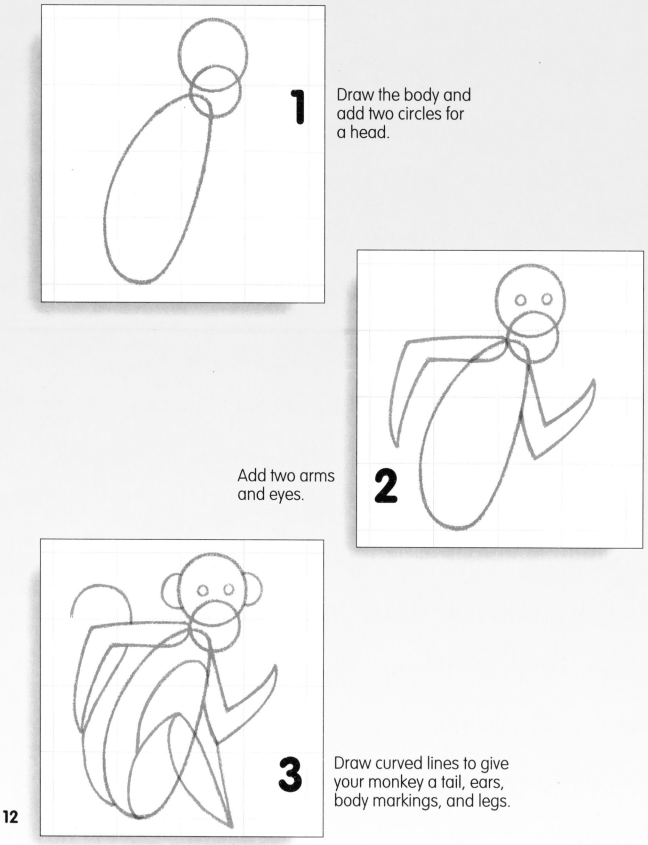

1 Draw the body and add two circles for a head.

Add two arms and eyes. **2**

3 Draw curved lines to give your monkey a tail, ears, body markings, and legs.

4 Give your monkey a face and finish the tail. Add hands and feet and a banana to eat!

Use your felt-tip pen to trace over the lines you want to keep, and erase the extra pencil lines.

5

6 Color your monkey!

13

Cat

1 Draw the body and add a head and tail.

Add ears, a hind leg, and two front paws.

2

3 Draw eyes, a nose, a mouth, and whiskers.

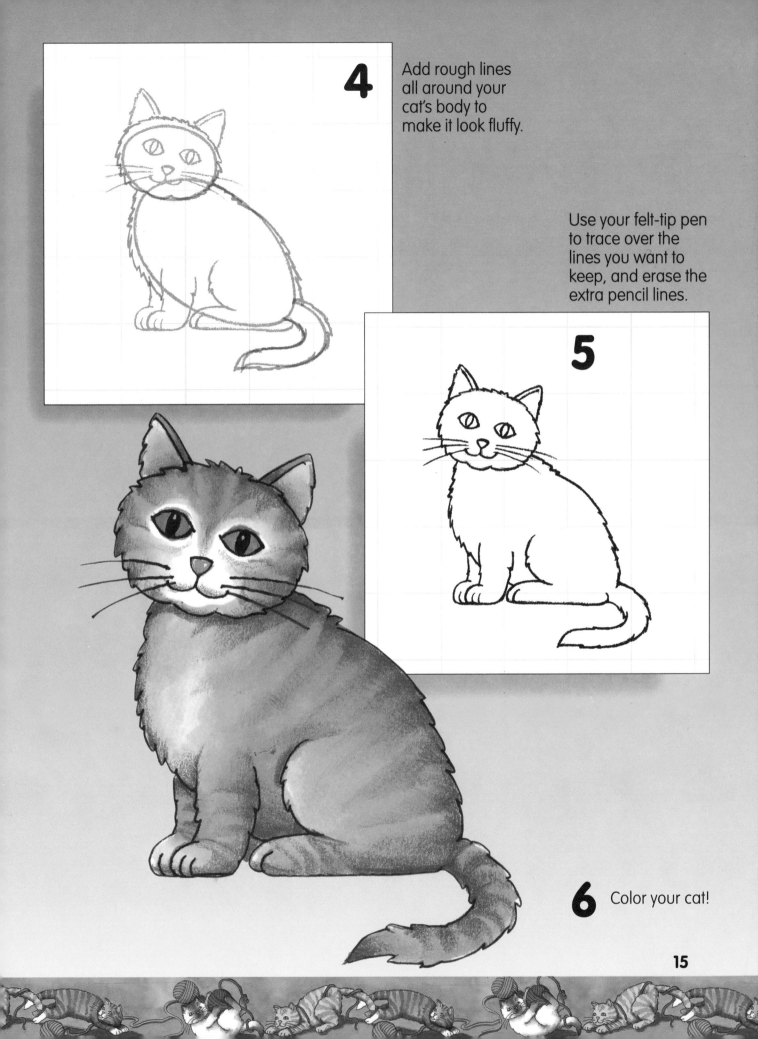

4 Add rough lines all around your cat's body to make it look fluffy.

Use your felt-tip pen to trace over the lines you want to keep, and erase the extra pencil lines.

5

6 Color your cat!

Panda

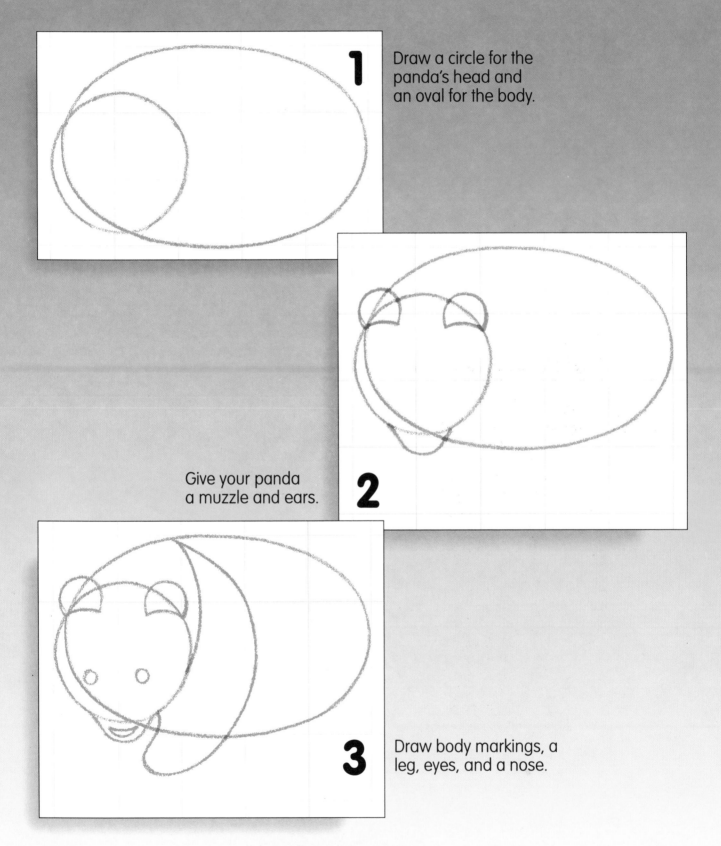

1 Draw a circle for the panda's head and an oval for the body.

2 Give your panda a muzzle and ears.

3 Draw body markings, a leg, eyes, and a nose.

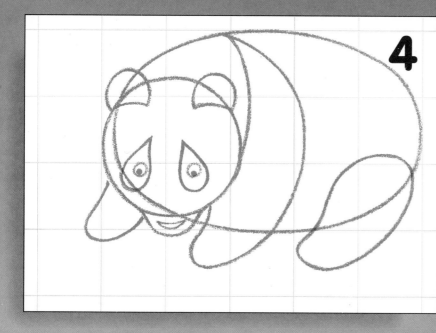

4 Add the other legs, the pupils and the eye patterns.

Use your felt-tip pen to trace over the lines you want to keep, and erase the extra pencil lines.

5

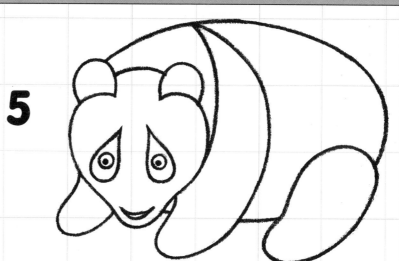

6 Color your panda!

rocks

bushes

iceberg

Making Backgrounds

You can draw backgrounds for your animals using the same kinds of drawing steps you've been using to draw your animals. These pages show some of the possibilities. Just start with basic shapes, and add the details one step at a time.

Learn to draw a bear on page 5. ▲

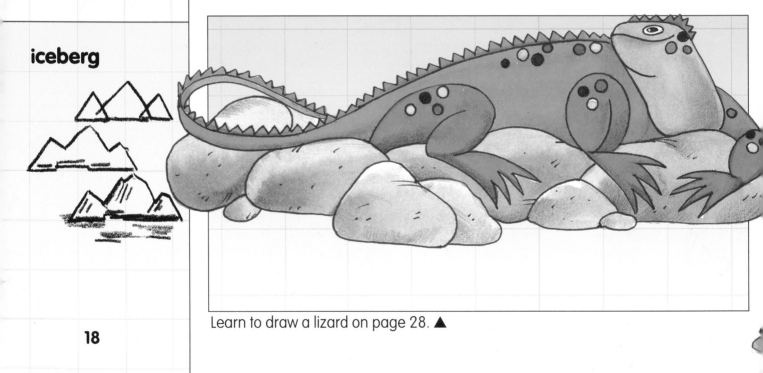

Learn to draw a lizard on page 28. ▲

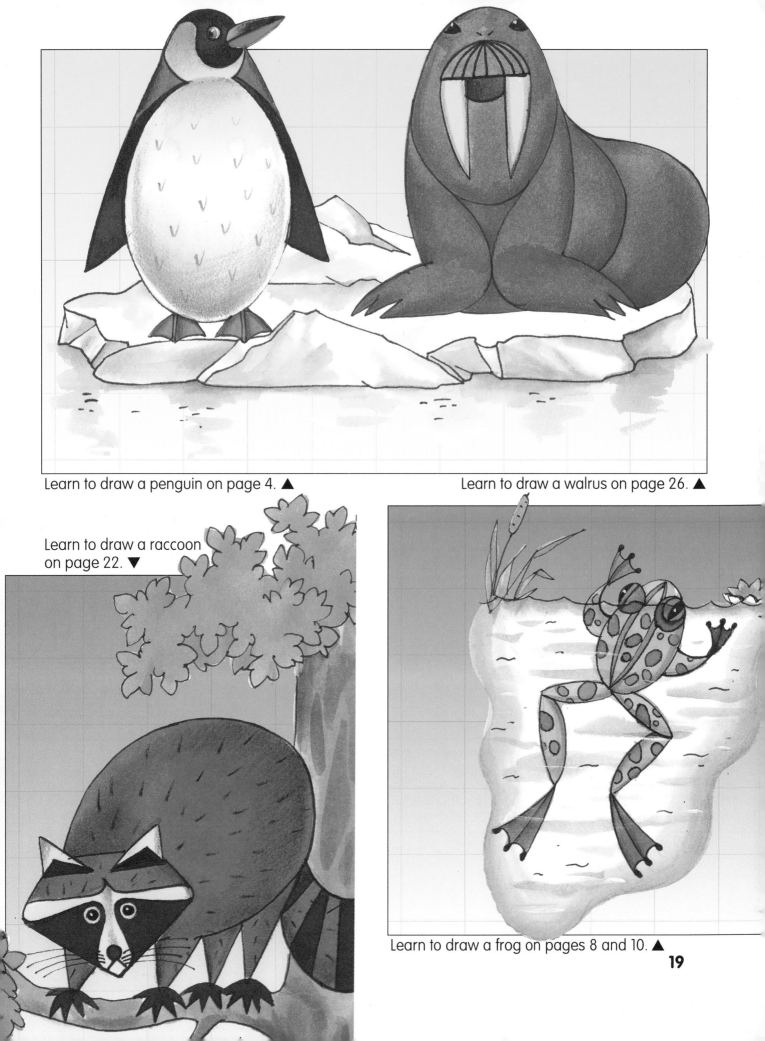

Learn to draw a penguin on page 4. ▲

Learn to draw a walrus on page 26. ▲

Learn to draw a raccoon on page 22. ▼

Learn to draw a frog on pages 8 and 10. ▲

Mouse

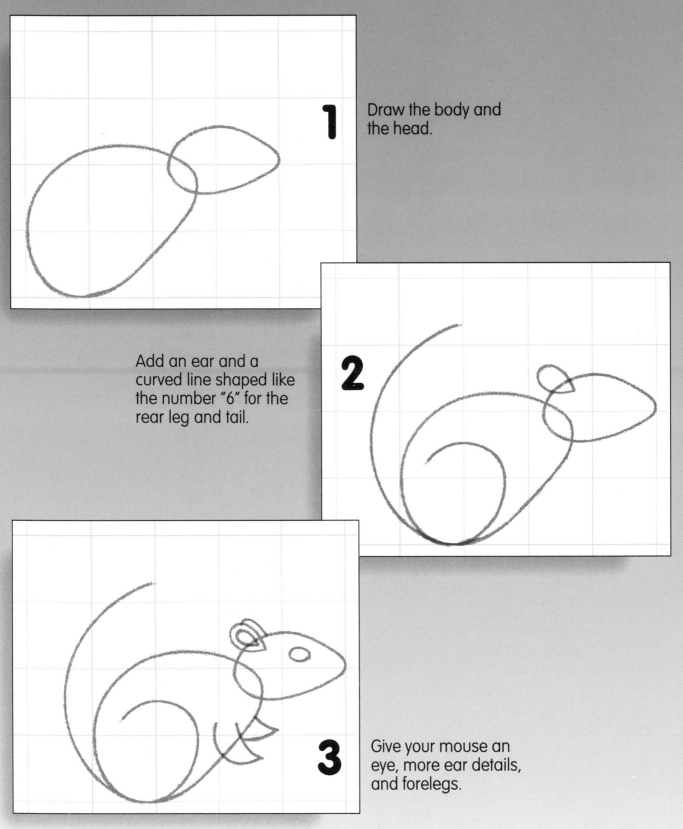

1 Draw the body and the head.

Add an ear and a curved line shaped like the number "6" for the rear leg and tail.

2

3 Give your mouse an eye, more ear details, and forelegs.

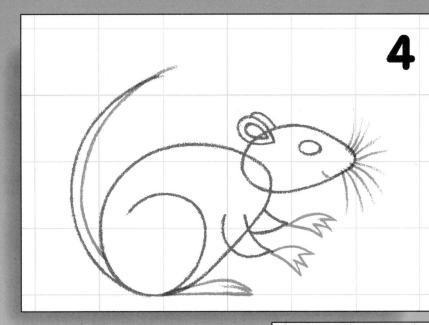

4 Add paws, whiskers, and a mouth. Finish the tail with another curved line.

Use your felt-tip pen to trace over the lines you want to keep, and erase the extra pencil lines.

5

6 Color your mouse!

Raccoon

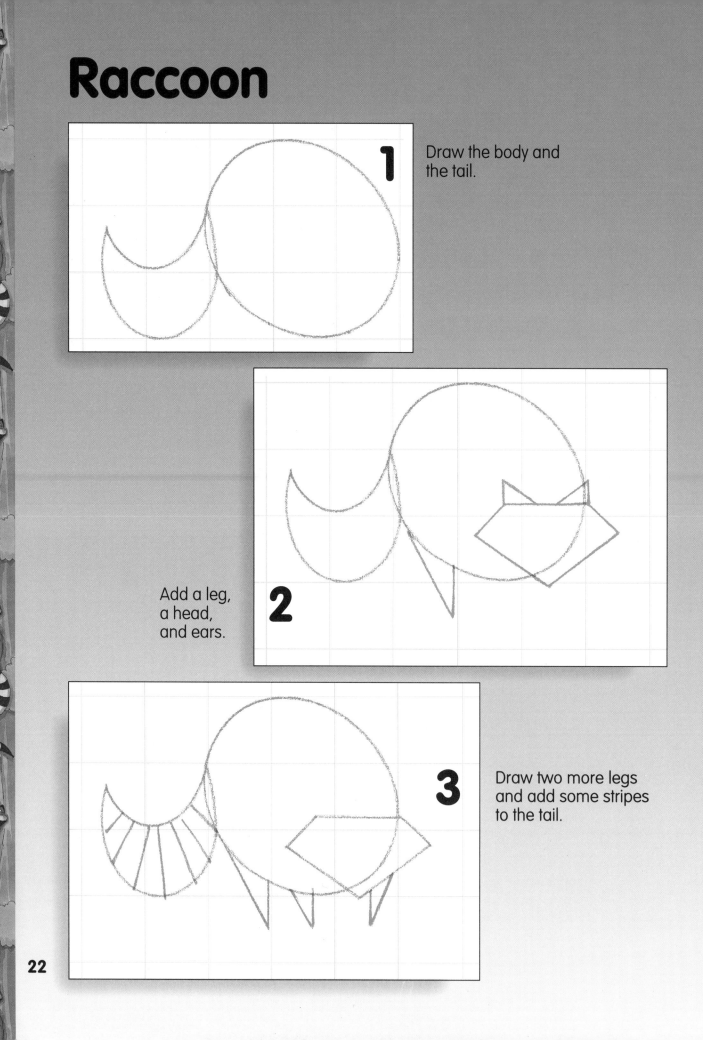

1 Draw the body and the tail.

2 Add a leg, a head, and ears.

3 Draw two more legs and add some stripes to the tail.

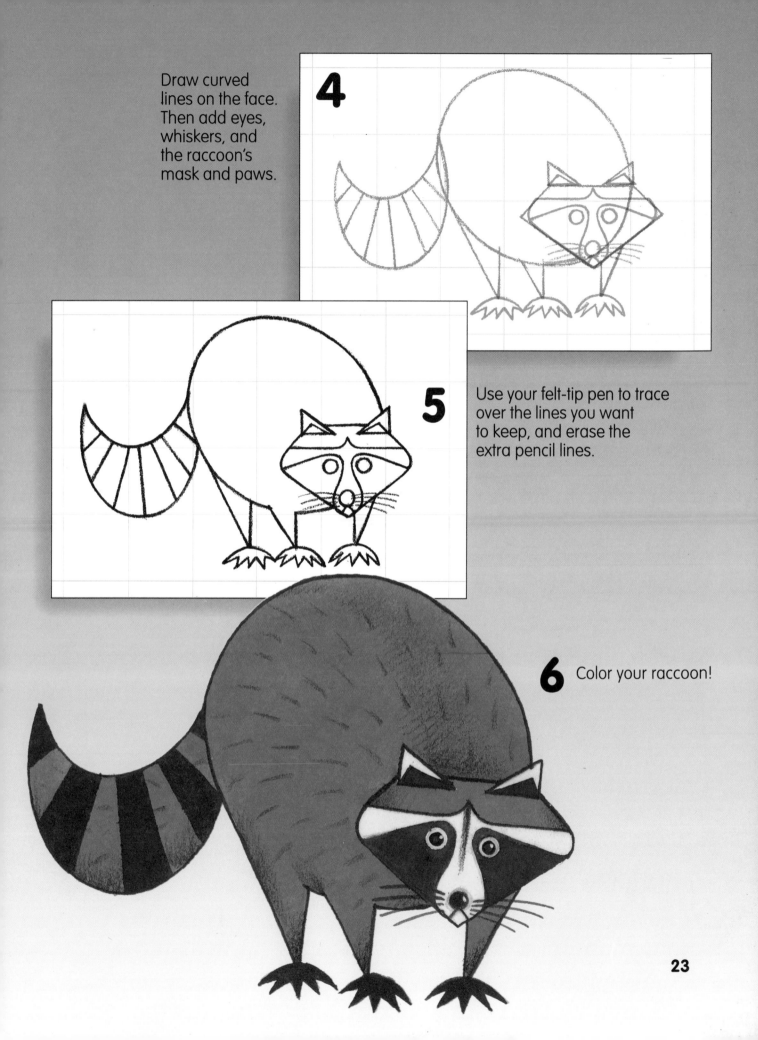

Draw curved lines on the face. Then add eyes, whiskers, and the raccoon's mask and paws.

4

5

Use your felt-tip pen to trace over the lines you want to keep, and erase the extra pencil lines.

6 Color your raccoon!

Walrus

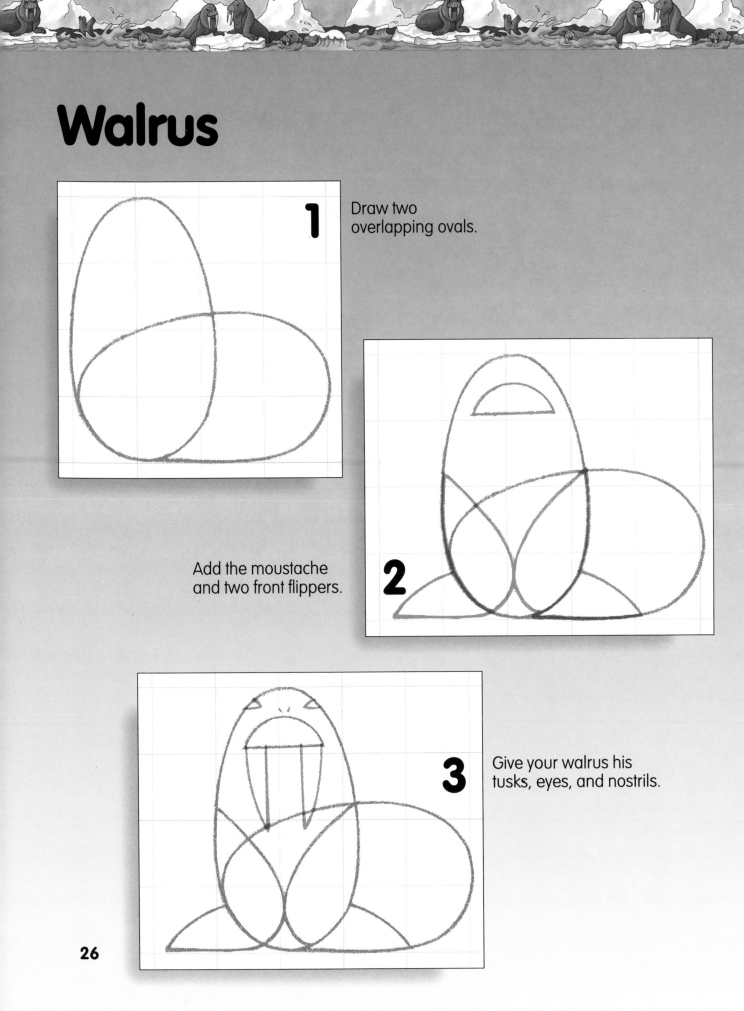

1 Draw two overlapping ovals.

2 Add the moustache and two front flippers.

3 Give your walrus his tusks, eyes, and nostrils.

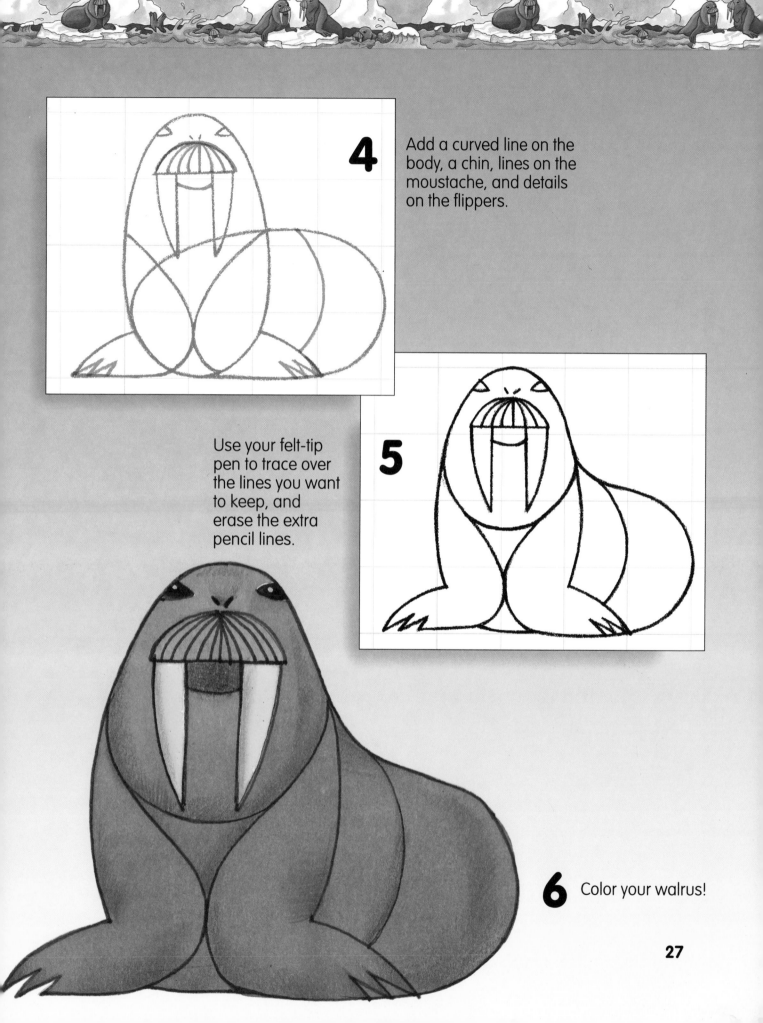

4 Add a curved line on the body, a chin, lines on the moustache, and details on the flippers.

Use your felt-tip pen to trace over the lines you want to keep, and erase the extra pencil lines.

5

6 Color your walrus!

Lizard

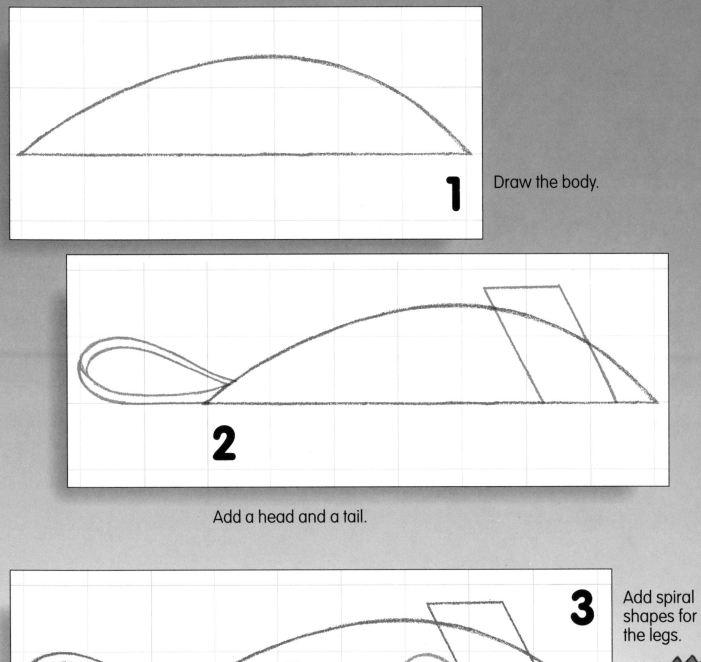

1 Draw the body.

2 Add a head and a tail.

3 Add spiral shapes for the legs.

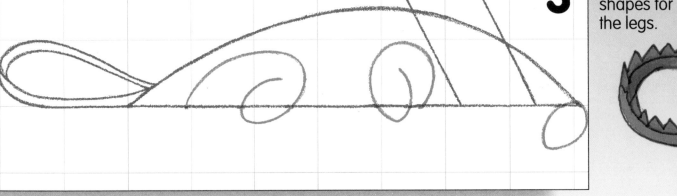

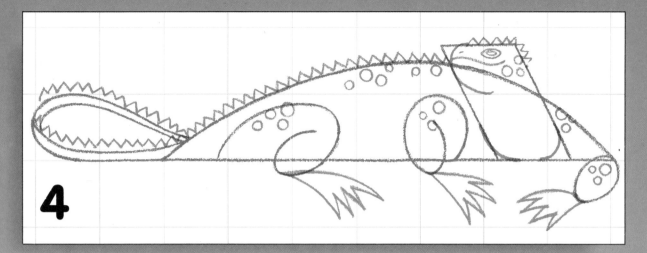

4

Draw zigzags across the back. Add feet, a face, a curved neck, and spots.

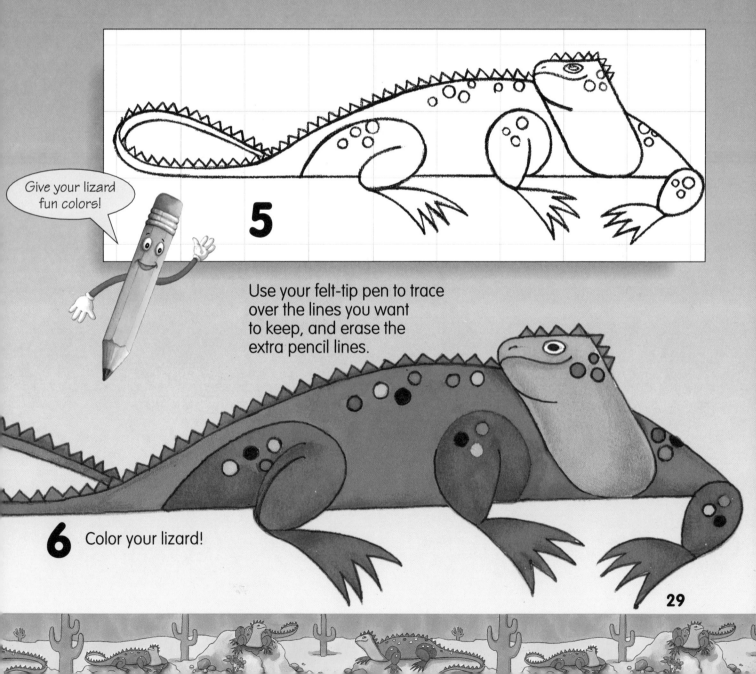

5

Give your lizard fun colors!

Use your felt-tip pen to trace over the lines you want to keep, and erase the extra pencil lines.

6 Color your lizard!

Coloring Your Drawings

Once you've finished the outlines of your drawings, it's fun to color them in. Use watercolor paints, colored pencils, crayons, markers, or anything else you can think of!

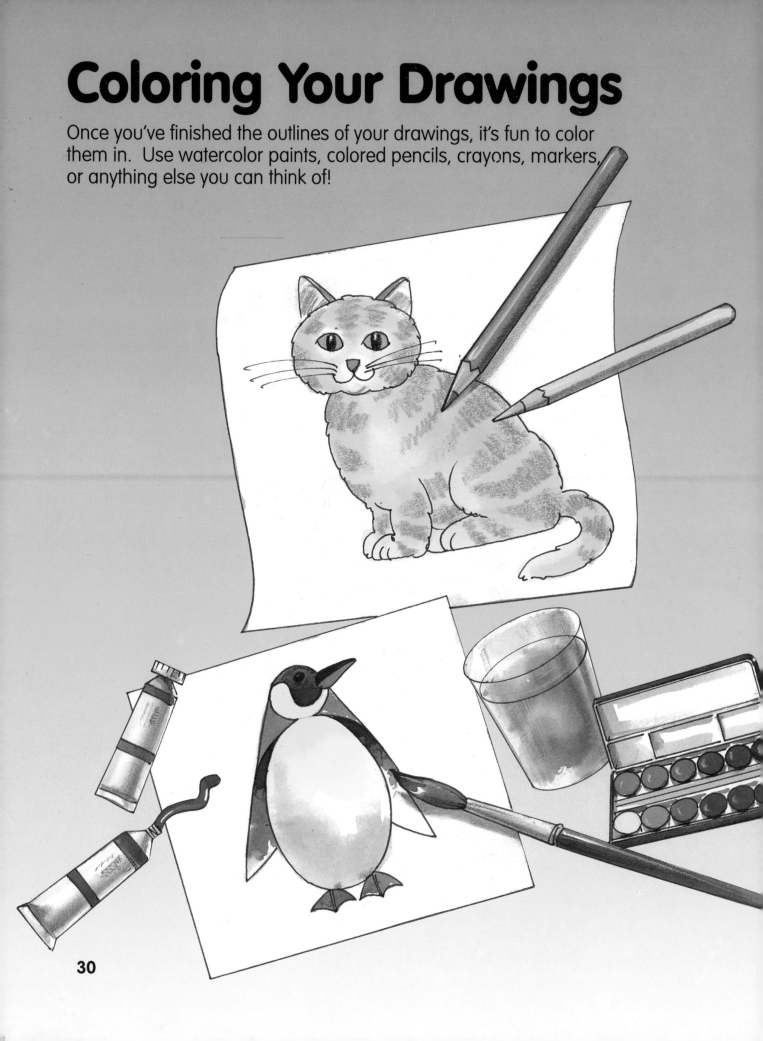

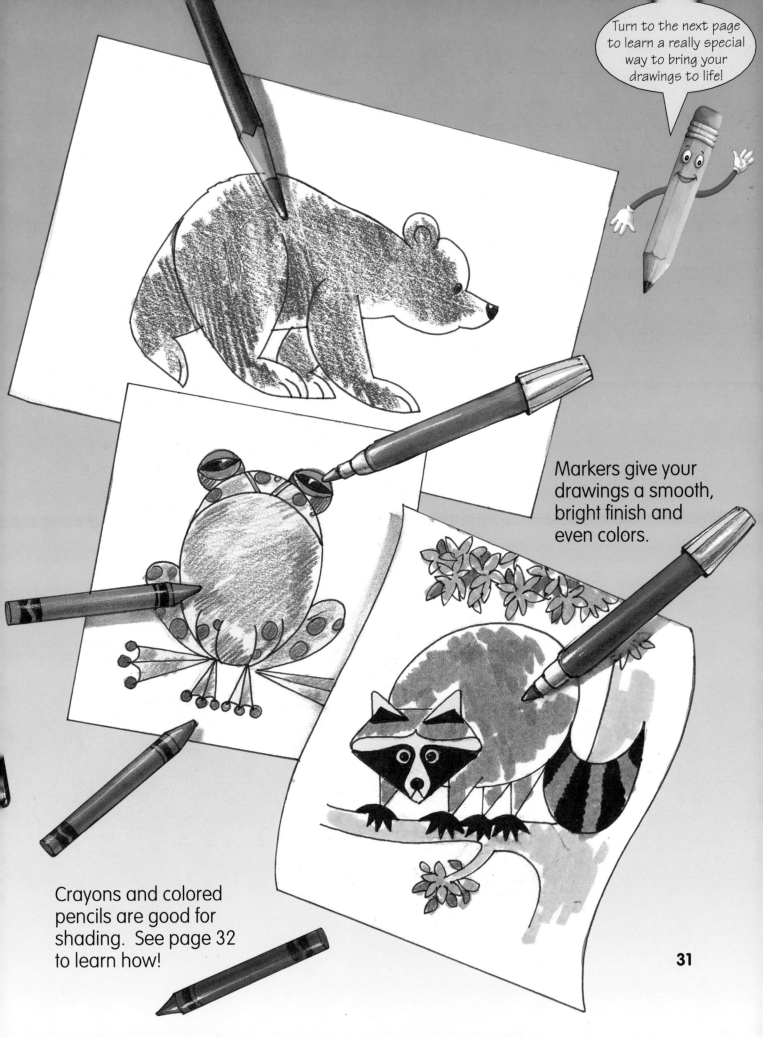

Turn to the next page to learn a really special way to bring your drawings to life!

Markers give your drawings a smooth, bright finish and even colors.

Crayons and colored pencils are good for shading. See page 32 to learn how!

Shading Your Drawings

Shading can add dimension and life to your drawings. Try shading first with a crayon or colored pencil, using the side of the point. Make an area of your animal darker where there would be less light on the animal. The darker areas create shadows, which give your drawing a 3-dimensional look.

Use these grid pages for your drawings. Make extra copies so you can draw lots of pictures using the special steps in this book!